MW00803105

SEP 28 2011
ROSSFORD PUBLIC LIBRARY
720 DIXIE HIGHWAY
ROSSFORD, OHIO 43460

j 597
GRE

FRESHWATER FISH

Tom Greve

ROURKE
PUBLISHING
www.rourkepublishing.com

© 2012 Rourke Publishing LLC

All rights reserved. No part of this book may be reproduced or utilized in any form or by any means, electronic or mechanical including photocopying, recording, or by any information storage and retrieval system without permission in writing from the publisher.

www.rourkepublishing.com

PHOTO CREDITS: Cover: © Krzysztof Odziomek; Title Page: © Toonman; Page 2, 3: © Verastuchelova; Page 4, 5: © David M. Schrader, Krzysztof Odziomek; Page 6: © US Fish and Wildlife Service, Reto Kunz; Page 7: © Krzysztof Odziomek; Page 8: © NOAA, Reto Kunz; Page 9: © Michael Wood; Page 10: © Wikipedia, miniature, Chelovek; Page 11: © AP Images - Suthep Kritsanavarin, Sander Camp; Page 12: © Danijela Pavlovic Markovic, Carol Gering; Page 13: © Brian Sak, George Peters, NOAA; Page 14: © Jeff Chevrier, Jeff Schmaltz; Page 15: © Fotografescu; Page 16: © Lane Erickson, Lukas Blazek; Page 17: © David Pedre, Wikipedia; Page 18: © US Fish and Wildlife Service; Page 19: © Christian Draghici, Milan P. Mihajlovic; Page 20: © John Anderson, Steve Mann; Page 21: © AP Images - Kyodo; Page 22: © Pierre Chouinard.

Edited by: Precious McKenzie

Cover Design by Renee Brady
Interior Design by Tara Raymo

Library of Congress Cataloging-in-Publication Data

Greve, Tom
  Freshwater Fish / Tom Greve.
    p. cm. -- (Eye to Eye with Animals)
  ISBN 978-1-61741-777-1 (hard cover) (alk. paper)
  ISBN 978-1-61741-979-9 (soft cover)
  Library of Congress Control Number: 2011924822

Rourke Publishing
Printed in the United States of America, North Mankato, Minnesota
060711
060711CL

RouRke PubLiSHiNG

www.rourkepublishing.com - rourke@rourkepublishing.com
Post Office Box 643328 Vero Beach, Florida 32964

Table of Contents

Chapter 1
Life Underwater: Hold the Salt

Millions of Earth's most **exotic** creatures live in a place where humans wouldn't survive – underwater!

EARTH'S SURFACE WATER

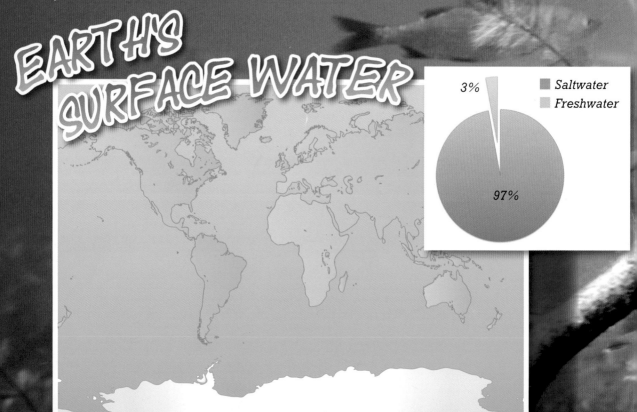

3%

Saltwater
Freshwater

97%

 Water, Water Everywhere: Water covers 70 percent of Earth. But less than three percent of it is freshwater. The rest contains high levels of salt, including all the water in the oceans.

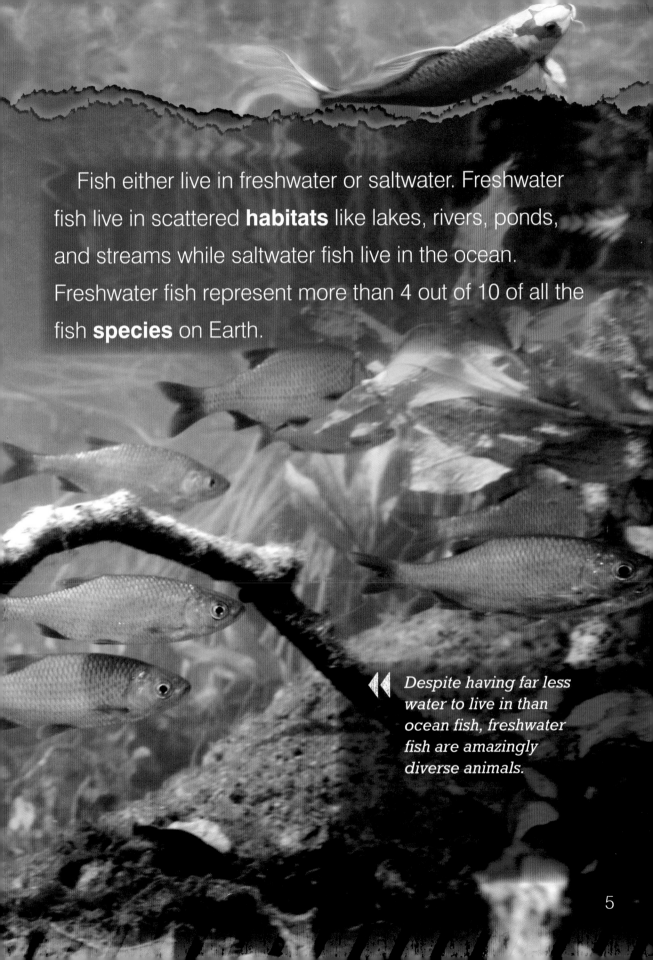

Fish either live in freshwater or saltwater. Freshwater fish live in scattered **habitats** like lakes, rivers, ponds, and streams while saltwater fish live in the ocean. Freshwater fish represent more than 4 out of 10 of all the fish **species** on Earth.

Despite having far less water to live in than ocean fish, freshwater fish are amazingly diverse animals.

Since fish live underwater, simple activities like breathing, moving, or even sleeping are different for fish than they are for animals that live on land.

Smallmouth Bass

All fish have a backbone. Scales cover the bodies of most freshwater fish. They are cold-blooded, so their bodies match the temperature of the water in their habitat.

Fish breathe underwater using **gills.** They move underwater by wiggling their bodies and using their **fins.**

Pike

FREAKY FISH FACT

Since their eyes are kept moist by the water, most fish have no eyelids. They sleep with their eyes open.

Many freshwater fish, like humans, have binocular vision. This means they see using both eyes. But fish eyes are commonly on the side of their heads, allowing them to see up, down, sideways, and back all at the same time.

Freshwater fish **adapt** to life in water that contains little or no salt. Most freshwater fish cannot survive in a saltwater habitat.

Salmon are a rare example of fish that can adapt to both salt and freshwater. Most salmon are born in freshwater rivers but then swim to the ocean to live. When they mature, they swim back up the river to lay their eggs.

Most freshwater fish have babies by laying eggs, a far smaller number of species give birth to live young. When fish reproduce, it's called spawning.

◀◀

Some freshwater species, like the Largemouth bass, are hermaphroditic, meaning they can be both male and female at the same time.

Unlike Earth's oceans, which are actually one large **interconnected** body of water, freshwater habitats like lakes and ponds are separate from one another. Many species of freshwater fish exist only in their specific habitat.

▲▲ *Golomyankas live only in the frigid waters of Russia's Lake Baikal.*

Lake Baikal

DEEP AND DIVERSE

▲▲ *Lake Baikal is Earth's deepest Lake (5,300 feet or 1,630 meters). Dozens of fish species in the lake live nowhere else on Earth. Its diversity even goes beyond fish. It is home to Earth's only freshwater seals.*

▲ Rivers also support diverse habitats. Asia's Mekong
River is home to the Mekong giant catfish. The river
has more species of large-sized freshwater fish than
any other river on Earth.

FREAKY FISH FACT

In 2005 fishermen in Thailand
caught a 646 pound (293 kg)
Mekong giant catfish. Roughly
the size of an adult grizzly
bear, it is one of the largest
freshwater fish ever caught.

Chapter 2

Freshwater Fish Food

Freshwater fish spend their lives as links in a food chain. Tiny plant organisms called **plankton** thrive on the surface of lakes and rivers where they benefit from sunlight.

Largemouth
Bass

Eagle

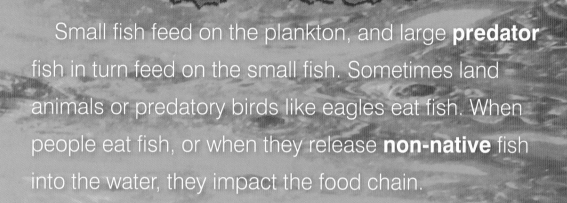

Small fish feed on the plankton, and large **predator** fish in turn feed on the small fish. Sometimes land animals or predatory birds like eagles eat fish. When people eat fish, or when they release **non-native** fish into the water, they impact the food chain.

Freshwater food chains can differ from one body of water to the next based on different species living in the water, in the air, and on land.

Algae Plankton

Zooplankton

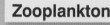

Sunfish

Chapter 3
The Great Lakes

The greatest concentration of freshwater on the Earth's surface is in the Great Lakes of North America. The Great Lakes are home to many different species of fish.

 North America's Great Lakes contain more than one fifth (21 percent) of all the freshwater on Earth.

▲ *The largest fish in the Great Lakes is the lake sturgeon. They are harder to find nowadays because fishermen caught or killed too many in the late 1800's. Sturgeon fishing is now illegal except for certain times and places.*

FREAKY FISH FACT

Looking like a freshwater dinosaur, sturgeon can be bigger than an adult human. Females can live to be more than 150 years old. There could be a sturgeon swimming around now that was alive during the Civil War!

Chapter 4
Fish Facts

Freshwater fish fall into two main groups.
In one group are fish that have jaws. This group is
divided between fish with bony skeletons, which include
most kinds of fish, and fish that have skeletons made of
cartilage, like sturgeon or freshwater rays.

◀◀
Trout have jaws and a bony skeleton.

▶▶
Freshwater stingrays have jaws and skeletons made of cartilage. They tend to live in warm tropical waters.

The second group includes fish without jaws, which include the **parasitic** sea lamprey.

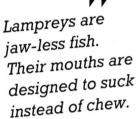

▶▶

Lampreys are jaw-less fish. Their mouths are designed to suck instead of chew.

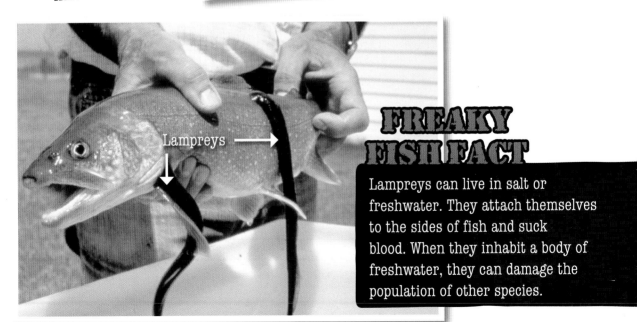

Lampreys

FREAKY FISH FACT

Lampreys can live in salt or freshwater. They attach themselves to the sides of fish and suck blood. When they inhabit a body of freshwater, they can damage the population of other species.

Chapter 5

Freshwater Threats and Conservation

Freshwater fish face threats from a number of sources. Lampreys are an example of an **invasive** species. They can adapt to new habitats and kill or eat too many of the fish or other food sources already existing there.

FREAKY FISH FACT

Invasive species can arrive at new habitats by accident. Asian carp were shipped to the U.S. to help fish farmers clean their ponds by eating algae. A flood overflowed the ponds into the Mississippi River. Because Asian carp reproduce quickly and have hearty appetites, they are a double threat to native species.

One notorious invasive species is the Asian carp. It has invaded rivers that flow into the Great Lakes. They multiply quickly and scientists worry they will eat too many native fish species in the lakes.

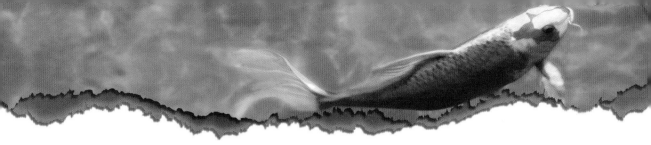

Man-made **pollution**, such as fertilizers, garbage, and industrial waste, also threatens freshwater habitats and food chains.

Man-made pollution ▶▶
makes the water unhealthy for the plants, plankton, and fish that live in the water.

DAM DILEMMA

 ◀◀

Dams are another man-made problem for freshwater fish. Despite their benefits in controlling floods and generating power, dams block fish from moving within their habitat to seek food or to spawn.

Governments and **conservation** groups are working to protect endangered species and their habitats from further damage.

Underwater electric fences can stop some invasive species from reaching into certain freshwater habitats.

Earth's freshwater ecosystem is fragile. Unfortunately, many freshwater fish species are endangered, and many more are already extinct.

FREAKY FISH FACT

In 2010, a Japanese salmon species thought to be extinct since 1940 was found alive and well. The black kokanee was found in a lake about 300 miles from its original habitat.

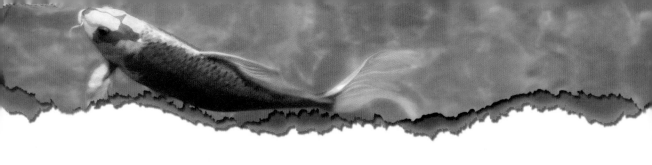

Flowerhorn fish

Freshwater fish are among the most diverse animals on Earth. Human factors like pollution have harmed some species. Keeping Earth's relatively small amount of freshwater clean is the key to sustaining the fascinating underwater world of freshwater fish.

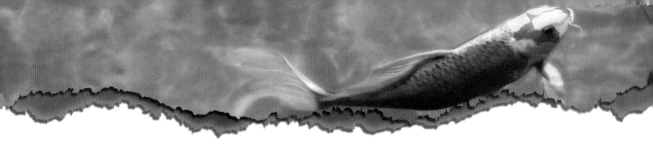

Glossary

adapt (uh-DAPT): change over time to accommodate a situation

cartilage (KAR-tuh-lij): strong, elastic tissue

conservation (kon-sur-VAY-shuhn): the protection of valuable or rare things

exotic (eg-ZOT-ik): strange and fascinating

fins (FINZ): body parts of fish that help it move and steer through water

gills (GILZ): internal breathing organs of fish

habitat (HAB-uh-tat): places and natural conditions in which animals live

interconnected (in-tur-kuh-NEKT-uhd): attached, physically joined

invasive (in-VAYSS-iv): prone to entering and taking over foreign places

non-native (NON-NAY-tiv): a person or animal from somewhere other than where they currently live

parasitic (pa-ruh-SIT-ik): animals that get food by attaching themselves to other animals

plankton (PLANGK-tuhn): tiny floating animals and plants that drift on the surface of water

pollution (puh-LOO-shuhn): harmful materials that damage or contaminate the environment

predator (PRED-uh-tur): an animal that hunts other animals for food

species (SPEE-seez): groups into which animals are divided and classified

Index

Websites To Visit

Nationalgeographic.org

epa.gov/greatlakes

WWF.org

nwf.org

marinebio.org

seagrant.wisc.edu/greatlakesfish

About the Author

Tom Greve lives in Chicago with his wife
Meg and their children Madison and
William. He loves the outdoors, and
grew up amid the many lakes, rivers, and
streams of northern Wisconsin.